TIGERS

A PORTRAIT OF THE ANIMAL WORLD

Lee Server

TODTRI

This book was designed and produced by TODTRI Book Publishers
P.O. Box 572, New York, NY 10116-0572 FAX: (212) 695-6984
e-mail : info@todtri.com

Printed and bound in Korea

ISBN 1-57717-080-6

Visit us on the web!
www.todtri.com

Author: Lee Server

Publisher: Robert M. Tod
Editor: Edward Douglas
Assistant Editor: Elaine Luthy
Book Designer: Mark Weinberg
Typesetting: Command-O Design

PHOTO CREDITS
Photo Source/Page Number

Erwin & Peggy Bauer 11 (top), 20 (top & bottom), 63 (bottom), 66 (bottom)

John S. Botkin 18, 21, 23 (top), 60, 63 (top)

Bruce Coleman, Inc.
Erwin & Peggy Bauer 59 (bottom)
Tom Brakefield 11 (bottom), 19, 27 (bottom), 30, 42, 68–69
Rolfe Kopfle 65
Len Rue, Jr. 70 (bottom)
Norman O. Tomalin 6, 29, 35
Rod Williams 47, 55

Dembinsky Photo Associates
John S. Botkin 12 (top)
Dominque Braud 4, 40–41
Russ Gutschall 33
Stan Osolinski 13
Anup Shah 3, 66 (top)
Terry Whitaker 54
R. Whittaker 49

Brian Kenney 10, 32 (top & bottom),
34, 37, 44 (left), 44–45, 45 (top), 50

Joe McDonald 22, 28 (bottom), 39 (top & bottom),
51 (top & bottom), 56–57, 61, 64 (bottom), 70 (top), 71

Mary Ann McDonald 11 (bottom), 16, 24–25, 27 (top)

Peter Arnold, Inc.
S. Asad 36
Gerard Lacz 48, 52
Ronald Seitre 31
Guenter Ziesler 38

Picture Perfect 23 (bottom), 62
Gerald Cubitt 28 (top), 67
Jack Green 8–9
Ron Kimball 26, 53

Len Rue, Jr. 15 (top & Bottom)

Tom Stack & Associates
Nancy Adams 59 (top), 64 (top)
Mike Bacon 46
Victoria Hurst 7
Thomas Kitchin 17
Mark Newman 58
Roy Toft 14
Dave Watts 5
Robert Winslow 43

INTRODUCTION

Despite its great size, the Bengal tiger is able to move through the forest in silence, stalking sensitive prey like deer without alerting them to its presence.

T he tiger is one of nature's masterpieces. A creature of beauty and grace, it rivals only man in its power and cunning. Whether encountered through the bars of a zoo's enclosure, or glimpsed in the wild as it stalks its prey with silent footfalls and eyes red as fire, the sight of this great cat is not easily forgotten. The tiger's body is thickly yet exquisitely designed, the steely muscles in back and shoulder rippling in movement, the huge legs propelling it so smoothly and quietly that it seems to be gliding above the jungle floor.

It is the largest of all felines, some measuring up to 13 feet (4 meters) long and weighing as much as 700 pounds (318 kilograms). Its powerful canine teeth, nearly the size of a man's finger, can kill even large prey in an instant, and it has been known to bring down adversaries as big as the elephant and the rhinoceros. When the tiger is own the prowl, the atmosphere in the forest is charged, and the air crackles with assorted cries of danger.

Until this century, the tiger was the uncontested ruler of its domain, an invincible predatory monarch. It reigned supreme not just in its legendary habitat, the wilds of India, but in the jungles and mangroves of Southeast

Asia, the snowbound conifer forests of Siberia, and the steppes and mountains beyond the Caspian Sea—across nearly every corner of the Asian continent from Turkey in the west to Korea in the east.

For the tiger, those times are no more. It is estimated that the tiger population before 1900 numbered in the hundreds of thousands. Today, after nearly a century of industrial development and the exploitation of vast tracts of former wilderness, the total world population of noncaptive tigers in their natural habitat has been estimated by some to be as low as five thousand, while others feel that eight thousand is a more accurate figure. However, through ever-increasing awareness and strong conservation measures, there is hope these numbers will increase. The fight for the tiger's survival grows stronger as more people learn the story of its treatment by humans, as well as the fascinating natural history of the animal itself.

Found mainly in eastern Russia and in parts of China and Korea, the Siberian tiger has been severely endangered by poachers. However since 1994, Operation Amba, a group of concerned Russian conservationists, has been extremely effective in combating this problem, and tiger numbers have increased.

The smallest of today's tiger subspecies, the Sumatran tiger is distinctive for being the only tiger to live in isolation on a large island. Located in the Indian Ocean southwest of the Malay Peninsula, the Indonesian island of Sumatra is home to many forms of wildlife, including elephants and leopards.

PORTRAIT OF A PREDATOR

While the tiger is most often thought of as a denizen of the tropical jungle, its actual origins are in the cold, snowbound areas of northern Asia, perhaps as far north as the lower Arctic. At some time in the ancient past, the tiger migrated south, throughout eastern Asia and the Indian subcontinent, and west to Turkey and Iran.

It has lived in habitats of great ecological diversity, and has evolved into a number of distinct subspecies, with individual modifications.

Tigers from the original northern habitat—the Siberian subspecies—are the largest tigers and have a considerably thicker coat to conserve body heat in the frigid winters of their homeland. Farther south, the tiger becomes smaller, its coat thinner. The Siberian tiger measures up to 13 feet (4 meters) in length, while the Bengal of India has an average length of 10 feet (3 meters). The island tigers of Sumatra and Bali, still farther south, have an average length of 8 feet (2.5 meters).

Although tigers living in tropical habitats have a much lighter coat than their Siberian cousins, the animals' northern origins are still felt in hot climates. The Bengal tiger tries to spend blazing hot days lying in shade or in cooling water. If forced to move around in the midday sun, the tiger pants heavily, its tongue hanging out. Curiously, the Siberian tiger's typical tawny and black striped coat is more appropriate for the jungle topography of the south, where it can blend in with the grass and undergrowth for camouflage, than for the white winter landscapes of the far north.

Following page: The Bengal, or Indian, tiger once populated vast areas of the Indian subcontinent, with a range extending from Pakistan to western Burma. Though now reduced to little more than 5,000 animals, it is the most numerous of the surviving tiger subspecies.

The massive Siberian tiger is the largest of all cats. This subspecies is also believed to be the one from which all other tiger types developed, as they migrated from their original northern habitats and eventually populated large parts of Asia.

The tiger is one of the world's most feared predators. Even in a relaxed moment, the cat's glittering eyes warn of deadly menace, and the tautness of the crouched, powerful body suggests the animal's stealth, speed, and power.

Though largely associated with thickly forested terrain, tigers also thrive in wet, swampy areas, that provide dense vegetation for cover and are filled with abundant prey. One of the most noted of these is the Sundarbans delta region of India and Bangladesh.

It is the Indian, or Bengal, tiger that makes the most flexible use of its coat and markings. The Indian subcontinent has a wide variety of landscapes and temperatures, from the snowy forests of the Himalayas and the swampy Sundarbans, to the parched scrubs of Rajasthan. The Bengal tiger has adapted to each environment. The tiger's color and markings amazingly serve as camouflage in a variety of geographical conditions. After seeing this distinctive animal unobstructed, with its bold color and unique pattern of stripes, it is hard to believe that it can blend in so efficiently in such a range of surroundings. In tall grass, the tiger's body matches the stalks, as its stripes become their shadows. In a bamboo forest, the tiger seems indistinguishable from the yellow trees. In the brown and yellow world of the deciduous forest, the tiger again is virtually invisible. Viewed from a short distance of even a few yards, a tiger is hard to spot. In the game parks, visitors are often dependent upon experienced guides to point out the giant cats, even when they are looking directly at the animal. Once seen, the tiger can shift slightly and disappear again.

While it may seem to the casual observer that all tigers have similar, even identical, coloration and markings, there is a wide, if relatively subtle, range of colors, and in fact no two tigers have exactly the same markings. even on an individual tiger, the markings of the right and left sides are different. Stripes may be thinner or become spots. The number of variations is infinite.

Similarly, there is no uniform color in the tiger's coat. The fur ranges from a very light orange to dark shades of red and ocher.

Certain areas—throat, chest, muzzle, stomach, and the insides of the legs—are colored various shades of white. The stripes may be reduced on the forelegs and shoulders. White tigers are rare—the first specimen was caught only in 1820—and white Siberians rarer still, but white Bengals have been found in many areas of India. Some are a dazzling pure white, with eyes of pale pink. More often they are an off-white with brown or black stripes and cold, blue eyes.

At first it was believed that white tigers were a separate race, but they are actually albinos with a mutant gene. They are born in a litter with tigers of normal coloration. Still, they have long been objects of fascination or even superstition. In the kingdom of Assam, there is a long-held belief that a person who sees a white tiger will soon die.

While lurking in the shadows of a dense forest or advancing stealthily by night, the tiger's black stripes make it difficult for the animal to be seen, even though it is moving.

The tiger's striped coat allows it to blend in with reeds and elephant grass. It can remain still and motionless concealed by such cover until a likely victim comes within range of attack.

11

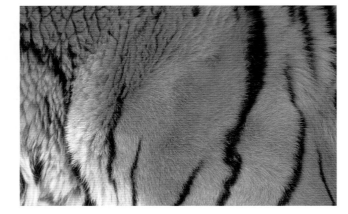

Fur coloration of the different tiger subspecies ranges from reddish orange to reddish ochre. Differences in the stripe patterns also occur, with some tigers having fewer and bolder stripes than others.

Classification of Tigers

Because the tiger is a solitary and elusive creature, it has been one of the least studied animals, and there has long been a degree of confusion over many aspects of the subspecies. It was once believed that there were many more tiger subspecies than are now accepted. Through the centuries, scientists have been uncertain how to classify the animal. It was initially called *Felis tigris*, then the genus name was changed to *Panthera*, because of the tiger's characteristic roundly contracting pupils and partially ossified hyoid, a bone at the root of the tongue, preceding the larynx.

Other scientists believed *Panthera* should be applied exclusively to the leopard and jaguar, the spotted cats. Some naturalists suggested that the tiger be classified as the separate genus, *Tigris*. Of the original eight commonly accepted tiger subspecies, three are now believed to be extinct.

Two young tigers fight playfully in a river. Though one has a white coat and the other does not, they are siblings. White tigers are born in litters with other cubs that have normal coloration.

Bali Tiger

Like the Javan and Sumatran tigers, the Bali was an Indonesian island tiger. It was rarely seen, and some questioned its classification as a separate subspecies, even though it was darker and had fewer stripes than the other Indonesians. The Bali tiger vanished within the last decade.

Bengal Tiger

Also known as the Indian tiger, the Bengal tiger is large, averaging 10 feet (3 meters) in length. It was once common on the subcontinent, but has become scarce in many regions since the late nineteenth century. It reached the endangered point in the late 1940s. As a result of the conservation efforts that began in the 1970s, there are now six thousand Bengals living in the wild in India, Nepal, and Bangladesh.

Caspian Tiger

Similar in size and color to the Bengal, the Caspian roamed the tiger's westernmost range, its territory including parts of Afghanistan, Iran, the former Soviet Union, and Turkey. This subspecies began dwindling in numbers in the 1930s and is now considered extinct, in spite of reports of a few individuals still living in a remote part of Afghanistan.

Chinese Tiger

Native to eastern China, the Chinese tiger's habitat has included forests and rocky mountains, and many once lived in caves along the Chinese coast near the island of Amoy. The Chinese tiger has been hunted to the verge of extinction, partly because of a vast market for a variety of tiger parts used in Asian rituals and medicines. Found in a few scattered pockets of wilderness and in captivity, there are now perhaps forty Chinese tigers in existence.

White tigers are the result of a rare genetic mutation. Individuals such as the one shown here are not true albinos, since the dark stripes are very prominent and the eye coloration is normal. Since they lack the usual orange-colored coat, they find concealment in the forest difficult.

Corbett's, or Indochinese, Tiger

Named after the famed hunter and author Jim Corbett, these tigers are smaller than the Bengal and their color is darker. The Corbett's tiger has short stripes, which turn into spots. It is distributed throughout most of Indochina in the modern nations of Thailand, Vietnam, Cambodia, in parts of former Burma (now Myanmar), and as far down as Malaysia. The Corbett's tiger has the second largest population in the world after the Bengal, with some fourteen hundred to fifteen hundred individuals at present.

Javan Tiger

The Javan—named after its homeland, the Indonesian island of Java—was similar to the Sumatran, but with a darker coat that had a larger number of black stripes that were closer set. A dozen or so of these tigers were known to exist in the l950s, but this subspecies is now considered extinct.

Siberian Tiger

Sometimes known as the Manchurian tiger, this is the largest cat in the world, with recorded lengths of over 13 feet (4 meters). The Siberian has a much heavier coat than the Bengal, with long fur measuring up to 21 inches (53 centimeters) in places. During the summer, the coat becomes shorter. The typical coloration is lighter than That of the Bengal, and the stripes are brown and narrow. The Siberian is a native of the cold, northeast regions of Asia, the probable original habitat of the tiger. It has been on the endangered list for quite some time, with only thirty or so animals known to exist in the wild in the 1930s. Due to conservation efforts and other factors, the population in the wild is now two hundred to three hundred. In captivity, Siberians have done very well and now number well over one thousand.

Sumatran Tiger

A native of the Indonesian island of Sumatra, this tiger averages 8 feet (2.5 meters) in length. It's coat is dark red with cream-colored areas and long black stripes, often in double layers. The Sumatrans have suffered from massive habitat destruction and uncontrolled hunting. Their total number has dropped by half in the last decade, years after the tiger's endangered status was known to the world. There are now five hundred to six hundred Sumatran tigers left in the wild, and their future is uncertain.

A pair of Siberian tigers share an affectionate and playful tussle in the winter snow. Though tigers live solitary lives, a mated pair will remain together for a brief period during courtship.

The tiger is one of the most adaptable of animals. It is able to survive in the frigid northern forests of eastern Russia, and is equally at home in temperate and tropical areas.

THE NATURE OF THE BEAST

The tiger is a hugely built creature with extremely powerful muscles. The head is rounded, with a heavy, vaulted skull. The tiger's ears are small and rounded. The large and powerful teeth are set in a jaw of enormous strength, giving the animal a bite of extraordinary force. The tiger's whiskers vary in density from males to females: longer and heavier in males, slighter in females.

Senses

Vision in tigers is acute, but only under particular conditions. The design of the eyes gives a wide-angle view, important in the forest with its crowded vegetation and narrow visibility, but the animal has difficulty discerning objects that are motionless. It can detect the slightest movement of another animal's ears, but if the other creature remains still, particularly at night, the tiger may easily pass by it. Luckily, for the tiger at any rate, most vulnerable prey are not smart or brave enough to keep from moving in the presence of the great predator.

Like all members of the cat family, the tiger has excellent night vision, an important faculty for a nocturnal hunter. The tiger has a round pupil rather than the vertical slit of the domestic cat, but nevertheless the eyes work much the same way in the dark. Like the camera lens that is opened or closed depending on the amount of light available, the tiger has its own layer of photoelectric cells, called a *tapetum*, which alters the size of the retina as the light changes. The notion that a tiger's eyes turn fiery red in the dark is a misconception

Excellent eyesight and hearing give the tiger the ability to detect its prey in dense forests. Even at night, it has no difficulty locating its victim and stalking it through thick vegetation.

Using its keen eyesight, the tiger judges distance and observes the behavior of target animals, trying to determine the one that will be easiest to take. The head moves back and forth, as the tiger makes a final calculation and focus before charging.

The eye of the tiger has long suggested cunning and cold calculation. The latter, in fact, is exactly the purpose of this all-important sensory organ. Both by day and by night, the cat can accurately gauge its surroundings and respond to both possibilities and dangers.

Tigers must sometimes defend themselves against their own kind. Fights usually spring from competition over territory or from one tiger trying to appropriate the other's kill.

based on the reflection of light from by the tapetum. This phenomenon is familiar to anyone who has shown a flashlight or other kind of light into the eyes of a nocturnal creature and seen the vivid red reflection that resulted.

Regarding the tiger's sense of smell there is some disagreement. According to a number of trackers and some naturalists, the tiger does a considerable amount of hunting by smell. However, the majority believe that tigers do not depend on their sense of smell to find prey, and that this sense is quite underdeveloped compared to their senses of sight and hearing. Experiments in the wild and in zoos have shown that little use is made of the olfactory ability and that tigers, unlike many predators and large animals, cannot detect the scent of human beings.

On the other hand, their sense of smell allows them to detect members of their own kind. Tigers ritualistically spray urine on certain boundary marks in their territory. While the strong-smelling odor lingers, other tigers may sniff the area and hurry away, realizing that they are in another tiger's territory. The pungent scent markings serve to prevent violent confrontations and to stake out the area in which an individual tiger can hunt without competition from its own species.

The tiger's most developed sense is undoubtedly its hearing, which is acute. Using this sense, the tiger is able to pick up the slightest sound in the forest and can distinguish the difference between the sound of a leaf rustling in the breeze and one being brushed by another animal. It can even recognize the noises made by different species, ignoring the animals it has no interest in, but coming to immediate attention when there is the sound of preferred prey. In the days when tigers were hunted by humans, the cats became familiar with the clatter made by the handling and carrying of hunters' rifles, and would turn and run at the first sound of the metallic weapons.

Sighting prey, this tiger is all concentration. It will be equally as keen when it hunts at night, since like all cats, the tiger's night vision is excellent.

A Bengal tiger sniffs a tree that has been sprayed with a strong smelling secretion by another tiger to establish a border to its territory.

The nostrils of the tiger are useful in detecting the scents of prey and in examining its surroundings. While their sense of smell is strong, like all cats, tigers rely heavily on sight and hearing for hunting.

Movement

The tiger walks in a characteristically graceful and nearly silent manner, seeming to glide as it moves. This smooth gait is due to the almost simultaneous movement of both the legs on one side of the body and then on the other. Some studies say that the tiger's steps are mathematically precise, the advancing hind foot meeting exactly the spot covered by the forefoot. Others have measured a fractional lag by the rear foot, showing that the animal steps consistently just behind the previous print.

The pads at the bottom of the tiger's feet are surprisingly soft and sensitive, and can be easily burnt or scraped open. The tiger, therefore, cannot move easily or at all on certain kinds of terrain. In a chase, the tiger's prey can escape by reaching ground with thorny undergrowth or bare rocks heated by the midday tropical sun. Tigers often must sit and watch while deer and other prey animals drink from a watering hole during the daytime, when the surrounding rocks would scorch the tiger's tender feet. Animals with hoofs, such as the sambar (a species of deer), are well insulated to prevent such problems.

Though they enable silent movement, the tiger's paws lack the insulation that those of other animals have. In areas where the rocky ground becomes broiling hot, the tiger cannot follow its prey and must leave it unmolested.

Tigers walk with characteristic grace. The smoothness of their gait comes from the almost simultaneous movement of both legs on each side of the body.

A young tiger rushes in for a kill. It may or may not be successful, and if the victim is not caught on the second or third try, the cat will most probably give up the chase.

Following page: With slow and silent progress, a tiger stalks its prey through the cover of tall grasses. When it finally attacks, it will most likely strike from behind. This habit has given tigers a reputation for treachery.

Such ironies are quite calculated by nature, intended as a means to keep an apex predator like the tiger from overkill, allowing the balance of nature to be maintained. If there were no physically imposed restrictions on the tiger, it might easily wipe out the wildlife in its area and cause its own doom. Only man has been able to ignore or outwit these natural checks and balances, with the result that numerous animal species have been hunted to extinction and our own habitat is increasingly dysfunctional.

Other limitations on the tiger's effectiveness as a hunter include an inability to maintain a chase. The tiger is not a runner like the cheetah, but a stalker, and makes only two, or at most, three springs at its prey, after which it usually turns elsewhere. Also, the fact that the movements of a tiger on the prowl can be sensed by many of the creatures of the forest, and provoke warning cries, makes the tiger's hunt for prey that much more difficult.

When the tiger has moved close enough to make a kill, it springs forward at great speed. In spite of its stealth and superb hunting skills, the tiger captures only ten percent of the animals it attacks.

While the tiger cannot sustain a long run, it is capable of leaping impressive distances. It can cover up to 13 feet (4 meters) at a bound, and there are instances of tigers making jumps across 20 feet (6 meters) of ground and scaling walls more than 6 feet (2 meters) high. Going downhill after prey, one tiger was recorded making a leap of more than 30 feet (9.25 meters).

Tigers are capable of impressive leaps, which they perform to cross barriers, to cover ground quickly, and as the final attack on a prey animal. The impact of the tiger's heavy body landing on its victim ensures that the animal will be subdued.

A tiger advances menacingly, the lower lip curling into a snarl as a warning. The ears are turned back and the head is lowered, both signs of aggression and a readiness to attack.

The tiger's paw print—the Hindi word *pug* is often used—holds a great deal of information. For naturalists trying to keep track of the tiger population in a given area, pug marks can tell a cat's age, sex, weight, and sometimes even indicate the animal's mood at the time. The track is actually traced and catalogued by gamekeepers as the most practical way of counting tigers and identifying individuals among them.

Each tiger's pug is unique, including the size and placement of the toes, the shape of the lobes of the pads, the top of the pad, and other individual factors. Although other aspects of the tiger would allow individual identification, such as facial markings and stripe patterns—both of which are unique to each individual tiger—these things do not lend themselves to practical research. The tiger is secretive and nocturnal, not an easy subject for visual or photographic identification.

Young tigers have been known to enjoy climbing trees, but this is not done by the considerably bulkier adults. Still, they are quite capable of the occasional climb, and have been known to scale trees in order to escape an unpleasant situation, such as an attack by wild dogs, or to try to reach prey. There have been cases of men climbing trees to escape an attacking tiger, only to be killed when the tiger followed them into the limbs.

This view of a Siberian cub running through the snow provides an indication of the size and power of the tiger's paws. Even without the claws extended, a swipe from an adult Siberian's powerful limb can be deadly.

A young tiger, crouching and snarling, seems ready to leap toward an intruder. As it matures, this tiger's fangs, or canine teeth, will grow to a length of 3 inches (7.5 centimeters).

Unusual Habits

Tigers are among the few cats that really like the water, and many enjoy swimming or lazily floating in the water on a daily basis. This is not necessarily an instinctive habit, since tiger mothers must teach their cubs to enjoy water. The cubs tend to make a comic spectacle as they go through the trial and error of swimming lessons. Tigers are good, strong swimmers, capable of swimming for over three miles without pausing. In parts of India and southeast Asia, tigers live a semiaquatic existence, spending most of their time in dark jungle rivers and swampy mangroves. They have even been known to swim from one island to another in Indonesia.

Tigers communicate with each other with a series of different calls. Roaring is a means of communication between males and females in mating season, and this sound is heard frequently during the actual mating act. Tigers in general are at their noisiest when the tigress is in heat. When two tigers meet under neutral circumstances they make a chuffing sound, which involves holding the mouth closed and snorting through the nostrils. In captivity, when a tiger has become devoted to a trainer or zoo worker, it will also make this affectionate chuffing sound.

Another curious sound the tiger makes is called a pook. Because the sound is similar to the cry made by the sambar, many naturalists believe that this is an extraordinary form of mimicry. By imitating the sambar's cry, the tiger could elicit a reply and thereby determine the deer's whereabouts. While unproved, a similar belief was held about the Siberian tiger by local hunters. The tiger was said to entrap female wapiti deer by imitating a stag's roar during mating season.

Most cats actively avoid water, but the tiger readily takes to it and is an excellent swimmer. In the tropical climates where most tigers live, they spend long periods in water, cooling off on sultry afternoons.

Tigers have a variety of different calls. Of these, roaring is their most spectacular form of communication. This sound is made frequently during mating and immediately after making a kill.

31

Since tigers have no aversion to water, humans in the wild often find themselves in danger with no avenue of retreat. Fishermen in India's Sundarbans delta are at risk both riverbanks and in their small boats in the middle of rivers.

Tigers will enter almost any river, lake, or stream, often for no apparent reason except the sheer pleasure of it.

Seemingly an exclusively forest animal, the tiger does quite well around lakes and in wetlands where a wide variety of food can be found. Besides the sambar, there are monkeys, peafowl, chital, and wild boar.

THE KINGDOM OF THE TIGER

Tigers are loners. They spend most of their lives in solitude. Tigers cubs and their mothers live as a family until the cubs can safely fend for themselves. Sometimes two or more tigers from the same litter live and hunt together for a short period after leaving the mother's den, but they eventually go off on their own.

Territories

Tigers stake out the borders of their territory with sprays of urine, and sometimes by marking trees with their claws. A solitary male tiger may take as his range a very large area that overlaps the range of another tiger. As long as the two tigers are not competing for the same prey, this does not necessarily lead to confrontation. Tigers tend to concentrate their hunt for prey to a few reliable places such as water holes, making their rounds several times a day until food is found. Unlike the outlying areas of the tiger's territory, these key places

Though the tiger and the lion have similar skulls, the tiger's head is heavier and more catlike. The ears are smallish and rounded, and the whiskers are much thicker on males than on females.

Two sibling Sumatran tigers walk as a team through the forest. Pairs of tiger brothers sometimes live and hunt together for a time after leaving the care of their mother.

A pair of tigers, at the edge of a stream, seem to have spotted a possible meal. Though they are solitary animals, except for a brief courtship period, tigers occasionally come together to cooperate in taking large quarry such as buffalo.

will be defended vigorously. A tiger, however, becomes less territorial when food is abundant and easily obtained.

The territory of one male tiger often crosses into that of several tigresses, allowing them to share common ground for mating. The tiger may mate with all of the tigresses with whom he shares territory. The male may also mate with just one of the tigresses again and again over a period of many mating seasons. In all cases, however, the male leaves after impregnating the female, and she cares for the litter on her own.

Among tigers, as among other species, two males sometimes fight over a female in heat.

In most cases, the tiger who found the tigress first will chase the interloper off with a few angry gestures. However, on occasion violence is unavoidable. A fight between tigers is a matter of ritual, with both animals exchanging a series of challenges, after each of which the other has a chance to back away. The cats stare each other in the eyes, then begin baring teeth and fanning whiskers. As the tension mounts, the cats begin to vocalize—first a very catlike hissing, and then muffled growls. As the growling becomes louder and angrier, the tigers begin slapping at each other with their front paws. When one or the other cat unsheathes his claws, the combat escalates, and the tigers

make bloodcurdling noises, standing on their hind legs and swinging wildly. The fight usually only lasts a few minutes, but some have gone on for hours. If neither tiger withdraws as the loser, the fight ends with one or the other tiger dead, usually from a broken neck. Often, the tigress wanders away during the fight and finds another male for her purposes.

Now and again, two tigers join forces to attack another animal. There are stories of a pair of tigers attacking an elephant, or teaming up to kill a buffalo, but if true, these incidents are uncommon. Although at the top of the food chain in the jungle, tigers sometimes end up as another animal's prey. They have been killed by crocodiles and by packs of Indian wild dogs. In the latter case, the vicious creatures surround the cat on all sides and wear it down with hundreds of bite wounds.

Death in the Wild

When dusk comes to the forest, it is time for the tiger to begin its hunt for food. The animal moves casually through its territory, checking the usual places where it can expect to find prey. One some evenings, the tiger may simply position itself in the grass cover near a water hole and wait for the deer or other animals to arrive.

Once the tiger has sighted prey it begins to plan an attack strategy. It does not approach directly, but circles around the animal. If the prey is moving, the tiger may scurry ahead and lie in wait. When closing in, the tiger becomes very careful, lowering its body close to the ground with the eyes focused on the prey.

The tiger raises and lowers its head, making final calculations of the distance and angle of the target. Then the cat raises its body and attacks. Charging forward at full speed, front legs extended, tail tautly erect, it springs into the air. If the tiger has calculated the proper distance from the prey, and the speed and lift of the spring, the predator hits its victim soundly with its heavy body. Often though, despite the careful calculations before the rush,

Many animals try to escape capture by taking to the water. Unlike other predators, the tiger easily follows its victim and in most cases can out maneuver it with great accuracy.

the tiger lands short and needs a second lift to reach the quarry. Landing from the first spring, the tiger touches the ground very briefly, only long enough to arch down and propel its body in the air again in a second spring.

This thoughtful preparation for attack is no guarantee of success. Long-term observation of cats in the wild has shown that they make a successful kill only once for every twenty attempts. Tigers are far from persistent. If the prey isn't caught by the second attempt, tigers usually turn away and continue hunting elsewhere. They will do this way even if they have gone several days without a substantial meal. When the tiger springs, it generally prefers to hit the prey from behind, which offers the best angle for its typical killing method. However,

a side or head-on approach will be made if necessary. When the tiger lands on the victim, it either collapses the animal or pulls it over. Simultaneously, the tiger digs its front claws into the prey's head and shoulders and holds it down, exposing the neck to the sharp fangs. As the prey collapses, the neck is jerked violently in an attempt to snap the spinal cord. The tiger uses its lethal canines on the exposed neck, with a deep and well-placed bite. If there is difficulty inflicting a killing bite, the tiger will press on the trachea and smother the prey. From the posture that tigers assume at this point, it was widely believed that tigers sucked the blood from their prey, but it is not physically possible for them, or for any cats, to drink in this way.

Charging through the shallows, a Siberian tiger takes deadly aim at its quarry. With eyes fixed forward, the cat's mighty shoulders and powerful legs propel it through the resistance of water without any loss of speed.

As the tiger nears its victim, it shortens the distance further by changing from a run to a series of long leaps. The cat seems to fly across the surface of the water, and the prey is soon taken.

Though essentially solitary creatures, tigers can be social. They meet, recognize, and greet other individuals in their general area, and if food is plentiful, they may share each other's kills quite peacefully.

A snarling tiger shows the impressive canine teeth with which it bites into the neck of its prey. The smaller incisor teeth between them are used to rip flesh from the bones of animals once they have been killed.

Attack Strategies

The precise killing method a tiger uses depends on many factors: the timing of the tiger's attack, the type of prey, and the experience and aptitude of the individual tiger. When attacking a large animal—such as a camel, buffalo, or elephant—the tiger may try to hamstring the creature first, disabling it and making it topple, before moving to attack the throat. The immense size of these animals does not put the tiger off, but given a choice it will go for a smaller, young adult elephant or buffalo.

Elephant and buffalo present special problems because they are so often found in herds. The tiger has devised a form of commando

A river or lake is no obstacle to tigers, who have no fear of either deep water or swiftly flowing currents. Excellent swimmers, they can quickly cross considerable distances.

attack in such cases. It sneaks around the herd, looking to pick off a calf that has strayed. Out of fear of attack from the herd, the tiger hits and runs, killing or wounding the calf, and then lies low until the herd moves on and abandons the dead or dying calf. It is a tricky business, and tigers have been killed by herds as they try to maneuver around them. When attacking an elephant, the tiger tries to rip open the animal's trunk, making it bleed to death. The hit-and-run tactic is also used on buffalo and rhinoceros calves.

Tigers have no trouble killing domestic cattle. This can become a serious problem for farmers living along the boundaries of a tiger sanctuary. Cows sometimes wander into the tiger's territory, or a hungry cat may slip into the cultivated areas. Such intrusion often produces angry reprisals against the tigers, even today when they are protected by law in India under all circumstances.

For such small prey as monkeys and jungle fowl, the tiger may use only its paws and razor-like claws. It was once believed that tigers would not eat carrion or another animal's kill, but this has proved false. Even so, the tiger can not really compete with the jungle's champion scavengers, jackals and vultures.

The tiger seldom eats its prey at the scene of the kill, but drags it to a preferred spot. The great strength of its jaws is evident, as it uses its mouth to drag even huge animals for great distances. One naturalist observed a tiger drag his prey for a full mile (1.6 kilometers). With a small- or medium-size kill, the tiger walks ahead, carrying it between the front legs or to the side; a heavy carcass is dragged backward.

A discriminating diner, the tiger takes up to a half hour to prepare the meal. Like a surgeon, it removes hair and skin, and tears open a section of the carcass from which to remove various body parts. It usually begins to feed on one of the organs—heart, kidneys, liver—and moves on from there, avoiding only the viscera and the rumen, the all-important first stomach found in grazing, cud-chewing animals. The tiger's teeth do most of the work. The cat uses its claws mainly for gripping the carcass, but the tiger's abrasive tongue is quite useful in scraping every piece of meat from the bones.

Tigers are quiet eaters. During a meal the only sound is of breaking bones. The big cat will take an hour or more over its meal, eating

This is a familiar scene to house cat owners. Like the domestic feline, tigers have an obsession with cleanliness and devote a good deal of time to thorough grooming.

from 40 to 90 pounds (18 to 40 kilograms) of meat at one sitting. On average, tigers need a daily intake of about 22 pounds (10 kilograms) of meat, but they have been observed consuming as much as 300 pounds (135 kilograms) in a single day.

A good-size kill may be stretched over several sittings. In this case, the tiger eats its fill, then covers the carcass and goes off to drink or sleep until the appetite returns. Then the cat returns for more, chasing off any scavengers that have appeared in the interim. Sometimes a tiger decides to prevent scavenging by sleeping atop the carcass. A large kill can last for two days, and the tiger will not begin hunting again until the fourth day. Tigers only hunt when they are hungry.

During the heat of the day, tigers relax and sleep, luxuriating in the shade. The tiger has nothing to fear except other tigers and man.

After a substantial meal, a tiger yawns before settling down to a long nap. In doing so, the cat provides a glimpse of the deadly biting and crushing power of its teeth and jaws.

45

Mating

Travelers encamped in the forest during tiger mating season have come back with tales as lurid and action packed as any adventure novel. The air becomes alive with a screeching serenade, the sounds of a tigress in heat and her male admirers. When the female's love cry draws more than one potential mate, the rivals confront each other, sometimes in a loud and violent battle. Later, the victorious male and his new queen mate, accompanied by more ear-splitting noises, a din that has been described as like "the caterwauling of a hundred midnight cats."

Although tigers pair off only for mating, during this period a form of marital fidelity exists between tiger and tigress. The male remains monogamous while courting one female in heat, seeing no other tigresses and remaining in close proximity to his mate. Tigers live almost their entire lives alone, so social graces do not come easily to them, and the first meeting between a male and female may be accompanied by a great deal of tension and much snarling and snapping. Gradually, things settle down and the couple begin to make the first series of "romantic" gestures toward each other. The tigress nuzzles, kisses, and licks the tiger. She gives him a series of love bites and rubs herself along his flanks. Becoming increasingly agitated, she snorts loudly and rolls on the ground with her paws in the air. The male watches this performance with what has been described as a surly expression. Then the tigress gets down on her belly, gently presenting herself to him. The tiger moves over the tigress and, roaring mightily, mounts her. As the tiger ejaculates, he lets out a sharp cry,

Two young male tigers groom each other. Though quite large, they are only six months old. It is at about this age that they begin to hunt with their mother and to learn the skills of stalking and attacking.

This young tiger appears to be posing for the camera at the base of a tree. Cubs are extremely frisky, exploring everything in their range. They are particularly fond of tree climbing during this phase.

and sinks his fangs into the tigress' neck. The female growls back and dislodges him, quickly jumping to her feet and confronting him. The tigress will slap at the male, sometimes scratching him badly, and there are more loud noises from both parties. Having chased the male back, the tired tigress stretches languidly on her side. The tiger gradually moves beside her again, attentive to her every motion. He begins sniffing her and offering tentative kisses, until she springs up and moves a short distance away. The tiger follows, the tigress presents herself, and the ritual begins again. It can be repeated fifty times and more in a single day, once every five to fifteen minutes or so. The actual length of each copulation is less than a minute.

This goes on for nearly a week, Tiger and tigress remain together at all times, moving restlessly through a small range, eating little. What prey they do eat may be caught by either the male or the female. At the end of the five- or six-day marriage, the pair go their own way, the male possibly going directly to another tigress in heat.

Birth

The period of gestation is approximately 105 days, with the tigress visibly pregnant in the last ten days to a week before giving birth. The tigress's mate does not offer any assistance in finding food or ensuring her safety during this last, vulnerable period. To give birth, the tigress finds a place with heavy cover—a cave,

A mother and her cubs nestle safely in a protected den, where the cubs will remain during early infancy. If the den is approached by any creature, including man, the tigress will defend her young ferociously.

hollow tree, or a shelter among rocks. She may have from one to a half-dozen cubs, Overall, the average litter size for tigers is three, with as many males as females produced in each new generation.

As the tigress is about to give birth, the she begins licking her vulva and then pressing down on her lower half. Waiting for the delivery, she either sits, with one leg raised, or stands, pressing down against the vulva until the first signs of the litter appear. As the cubs are born, the tigress frees them from the umbilical cord and cleans them with her tongue. Tiger cubs are born blind. A few minutes after birth they begin to cry and then move sightlessly toward the mother's nipples.

A newborn tiger weighs around 2 to 3 pounds (780 to 1,600 grams) and measures approximately 18 inches (45 centimeters) from the head to the tip of the tail. Nine months later the cub will weigh well over 100 pounds (45 kilograms).

With her first litter a tigress may be awkward or uncaring for her newborn, frightened by what her body has produced. By the second and third litter, however, the same tigress will be a devoted and selfless parent. The notion that a tigress will sometimes eat her young has never been substantiated.

Tiger cubs are blind or nearly sightless for their first two months. This allows the mother to keep them under control and

Play is important to young tigers, for it teaches them the skills they will need as adults to hunt and to defend their territories. These mock battles, though fiercely energetic, are quite harmless.

Though this feisty young cub seems to be an independent spirit, it must completely rely on its mother for food until it is about a year old and can hunt on its own.

prevents them from wandering away while she is out hunting food. When the cubs are three months old, they can begin to move around with the mother, eating from her kill, and enjoying bouts of playful romping There is usually a great deal of physical affection exchanged between a mother and her young.

The tigress takes seriously her responsibility for teaching the cubs everything they must know for survival. She introduces them to the rudiments of stalking with games of hide-and-seek and encourages them to practice pouncing by trying to catch her shifting tail. In the first months, the tigress continually moves her family from one lair to another, to keep the cubs safe from other predators or even from male tigers. Any intrusion upon the lair will provoke a vicious response from the tigress. Many humans moving through the forest have lost their lives by unwittingly walking too closely to a place where a mother is protecting her young.The mother continues to care for her cubs until they are one or two years old. At that time the young tigers go off on their own.

A proud mother guards her two cubs. They will stay close to her until they are able to hunt and defend themselves. The mother's protection is vital, since even other tigers are a threat to her young until they are grown.

A tigress carries her cub to safety in the way typical of all cats. Although this appears to be painful, the loose skin around the neck is the ideal place for a cub to be held.

These tiger cubs are being cared for exclusively by their mother, who will teach them all the skills they will need for survival. Like all male tigers, the father left the tigress shortly after mating and will play no part in raising his offspring.

In spite of all the care and protection given to them by their mothers, almost half of all cubs born in the wild do not survive their first two years. Those that do have an average life span of twenty-six years.

Even at play, the superior leaping capability of tiger cubs is evident. With every jump, this young Siberian is strengthening muscles and improving the ability to gauge distances and cover ever increasing areas of ground.

MAN AND TIGER

History records that hunting big cats for sport goes back at least to the time of the pharaohs, over three thousand years ago. The ancient Assyrians kept lions and tigers in menageries and hunted them with bow and arrow from horse-drawn chariots. In Rome, the bloody battles between tigers and gladiators were the most spectacular and popular events of the arenas.

The courts of oriental kings used tigers as executioners. One Burmese ruler kept a park stocked with hungry tigers, to which he would condemn criminals. Marco Polo wrote of tigers used for similar purposes in the Cathay of Kublai Khan.

In other Asian countries they were baited and tortured for sport and finally killed by large packs of wild dogs. These bloody uses no doubt sprang from man's perception of the tiger as a creature of wanton cruelty. Often, over time, it was compared unfavorably to the majestic African lion. To human eyes, the tiger appeared to be forever scowling and perhaps plotting some treachery. This idea was reinforced by the animal's habit of taking its prey from behind, which was considered not only treacherous but cowardly.

Man-Eaters

The tiger's reputation as a man-eater comes not only from reaction to the animal's ferocity, but from the records of thousands of people killed over the years. While humans are not the natural prey of this animal, various circumstances can lead to tiger attacks. It is believed that sick or injured tigers, unable to capture the large animals they prefer, are forced to take the smaller humans. This can lead to the tigers acquiring a taste for human flesh, causing them to continue to attack people and become man-eaters.

Conservation efforts in India have proven extremely beneficial for the tiger. However, local villagers living close to tiger preserves have found that the danger of tiger attacks on humans has increased dramatically.

Since the days of the Roman Empire, written accounts of the tiger have dwelt on its awesome combination of great beauty and ferocity. Commonly thought to be wantonly cruel, it has been understandably feared as a man-eater.

Deep snow and freezing temperatures cause no discomfort to this magnificent Siberian tiger. Its long, thick fur is adequate protection from the elements and keeps the winter cold at bay.

This quiet, almost benign, portrait of a tiger belies the fact that this cat species is responsible for more human deaths than any other predator in the animal kingdom.

In spite of this possibility, humans continue to move into tiger territories, pushed by the economic necessities of a growing population, to find new areas for agriculture and forestry. Inevitably, casualties occur as humans and tigers come into conflict. Fortunately, though there is definite danger, tiger attacks are considered rare in most of Asia.

The exception to this is in the Sundarbans river delta region of India and Bangladesh. About 250 tigers live in this 4,000 square mile (10,360 square kilometer) area of thick forests and mangrove swamps. Though the Sundarbans uninhabited, people enter to tap the area's rich store of fish, honey, and certain woods. The fishermen and foragers know that this is hazardous work, for the tigers of the

Sundarbans have developed a strong tendency to attack humans, causing a number of deaths each year. When an attack comes, it is sudden and swift. Anyone wandering alone in the forest is at great peril, as is the last person in a group walking single file through the trees. Since tigers are excellent swimmers, the river bank can be as dangerous as the forest, and even small boats in the middle of a river can become targets.

Standing on its hind legs, a tiger pulls its claws through the bark of a tree to mark a boundary of its territory. This practice is not consistent among tigers; some do it regularly, others not at all.

Need For Conservation

As human populations have grown, and business and government interests have moved in search of new resources, the tiger's wilderness domain has been disrupted and often destroyed. For many years, the killing of wildlife and the clearing of forests were considered marks of progress in primitive areas. However, even the mere thinning of forests for timber in parts of India has been sufficient to interfere with the delicate balance of the ecosystem, in which each component of the environment is dependent upon the others.

One of the many benefits of today's wildlife reserves is the opportunity provided to skilled nature photographers from around the world to capture such striking images as this photo of two fighting tigers.

Since so few Siberian tigers exist in the wild and an increase in their numbers is still uncertain, naturalists must continue to work to ensure that the Siberian's gene pool is varied enough to produce healthy young.

Today India has a total of eighty wildlife parks, some more accessible than others. Tigers can be found in many of them, along with an array of other creatures. Visits to a few of these preserves will impress the observer with the varied range of habitats in which tigers can thrive.

Though tigers do not grow manes as lions do, older tigers have ruffs of long, thick hair on their cheeks. In fact lions and tigers have much in common— the closest kin in the cat family.

Many modern zoos, such as the one in San Francisco shown here, try to recreate, as much as possible, the look of the natural habitats from which their animals come. Ironically, some tiger subspecies are more numerous in captivity than they are in the wild.

While the tiger has proven adaptable to certain changes in its habitat, it has been hard pressed by the massive upheavals of the past fifty years. In India for example, the amount of forested land has dropped from over 75 percent of the total land area to less than 20 percent. The tiger, as a solitary creature, designed to survive in its own defined, individual territory, is doomed by this situation. The shrinking of suitable habitat obviously leads to decline in the tiger population.

Signs of the tiger's threatened existence were known for some time, but ignored. Although a few tiger reserves had been set up in the 1930s, it was not until the 1970s, in response to worldwide alarm over the bleak prospects for the tiger's survival, that drastic action was taken. Conservation groups joined with the Indian government to alleviate many of the problems by organizing a highly successful effort known as Project Tiger. In addition, tiger reserves were created, with lands set aside that preserved entire environments. These were planned as core areas, places where human beings were forbidden to live or work. Just outside the core areas, buffer zones were designated, to which people had limited access to carry on certain regulated activities that posed no threats to wildlife. The project had a twofold benefit, for in saving the tiger, it also ensured the survival of other endangered animals.

Watching Tigers

India's tiger reserves are located in various regions of the country, representing every type of terrain. Many are easily accessible to travelers, while others are more remote. In all cases, the reserves provide an exciting opportunity to see the big cats living normally in their native habitats, with regulations strictly enforced to avoid violent contacts between humans and tigers. These rules, as well as warnings of all kinds, should be observed. Visitors should remember that wildlife parks are not amusement parks, and that a trip through a wild area requires a degree of caution.

In the following pages some of the leading tiger reserves of India and Nepal are described. While tourist facilities and accommodations vary from place to place, all wildlife areas are maintained in a condition as close to the natural state as possible.

Due to the success enjoyed by Project Tiger since its founding in 1972, youngsters like this Bengal cub stand a stronger chance of survival in the wild. Many of them may live to increase the numbers of their species further.

Corbett National Park was the launch site for Project Tiger in 1973. Filled with a wide range of animal species, the park is home to such big cats as tigers and leopards, and to such lesser ones as leopard cats, jungle cats, and fishing cats.

Kanha National Park in central India shelters twenty-two species of mammals and two hundred bird species. On of the finest Indian parks, it attracts bird watchers from around the world, as well as many others who come to see its prime attraction, the tiger.

Corbett National Park

Established in 1936 and named after naturalist-author Jim Corbett, this was India's first important national park. It is located in the state of Uttar Pradesh in Patlidun Valley at the base of the Himalayas. Approximately one hundred tigers live here, along with four species of deer, the big cats' favorite prey There is also a substantial leopard population, which stays as far from the tigers as possible. Visitors may observe wildlife in the safest and most natural way, from the back of an elephant.

Indravati National Park

Located in the state of Madhya Pradesh, the park has been associated with Project Tiger since 1983. Its core area of nearly 500 square miles (1,295 square kilometers) contains huge expanses of teak and bamboo forests, and is an important home for water buffalo as well as for tigers.

Kanha National Park

Kanha, also in Madhya Pradesh, is a rich green area of forests and valleys, parts of which have been a sanctuary since the 1930s. Project Tiger has done much to make this a thriving area for tigers and other major species. A successful relocation program moved a large number of villages out of the park, and today Kanha is regarded as the greatest of all the Indian parks.

Namdapha National Park

Namdapha is in the state of Arunachal Pradesh close to the border with China, and is the northeasternmost domain of the Bengal tiger. With high areas of alpinelike forests some 15, 000 feet (4,575 meters) above sea level, it is the only park that contains India's three major predators: the leopard, the clouded leopard, and the tiger. Since it is in a remote, inaccessible part of the country, Namdapha is little visited and therefore completely unspoiled.

From a rocky vantage point, a tiger keeps watch on its surroundings in Kanha National Park. Green and hilly, the park is known as the best place in the world to observe tigers.

Living in a wildlife reserve in southern Sumatra, this Sumatran tiger is one of the few survivors of its kind. Though they are rich in wildlife, Indonesian parks can only be visited by people who are able to gain special permission.

This is a typical view as seen by visitors to Ranthambhore National Park in India. The tigers in this park are relatively abundant and many are active during the day.

Ranthambhore National Park

This park, in the arid state of Rajasthan, is perhaps the best location of all for seeing tigers. Here, they have lost their shyness or fear of humans and, uniquely, are quite active during the day and sometimes can even be seen hunting prey. The park's site was once the center of a fourteenth-century Hindu kingdom, and a few of Ranthambhore's forty tigers can often be seen climbing among the ruins of its historic fort.

Royal Chitwan National Park

Formerly a hunting ground for Nepal's ruling family, the park covers a pristine area of hilly woodlands, lakes, and flood plains in southern Nepal, 75 miles (120 kilometers) southwest of Kathmandu. It is home not only to the tiger and a significant deer population, but to a number of endangered animals, including the one-horned rhinoceros, Gharial crocodile, pangolin, and Gangetic dolphin.

The Future of the Tiger

Increased understanding of environmental problems combined with the growing economic importance of tourism has led to greater support for the creation and maintenance of parks and reserves. Since the inception of Project Tiger in 1973, the Indian tiger population has doubled, and nineteen tiger reserves have been established, covering 11,470 square miles (29,716 square kilometers) of forest area. However, this progress has been undercut by poaching, which is believed to claim the lives of several hundred tigers each year in Asia. Concerned wildlife and government interests have been increasingly involved in solving this problem in recent years.

Difficulties such as this will continue to arise, but, though it is too soon to declare victory for the tiger, there is a growing probability that this magnificent animal will survive, for a world without tigers would be a poor place indeed.

This Siberian tiger is resting atop the snow in the warm afternoon sun. Soon it will be up again and roaming the forest in search of prey, the never-ending challenge of life in the wild.

Strolling down a well worn road in India's Ranthambhore National Park, a tiger surveys its domain, which it shares with large numbers of tourists each year

INDEX

*Page numbers in **bold-face** type indicate photo captions.*